LAWS AND LEGISLATION

INSPECTORS GENERAL

OVERVIEW, INDEPENDENCE AND EFFECTIVENESS

LAWS AND LEGISLATION

Additional books in this series can be found on Nova's website under the Series tab.

Additional E-books in this series can be found on Nova's website under the E-book tab.

CONGRESSIONAL POLICIES, PRACTICES AND PROCEDURES

Additional books in this series can be found on Nova's website under the Series tab.

Additional E-books in this series can be found on Nova's website under the E-book tab.

LAWS AND LEGISLATION

INSPECTORS GENERAL

OVERVIEW, INDEPENDENCE AND EFFECTIVENESS

Anderson Lewis
and
Todd F. Hill
EDITORS

Nova Science Publishers, Inc.
New York

For permission to use material from this book please contact us:
Telephone 631-231-7269; Fax 631-231-8175
Web Site: http://www.novapublishers.com

Library of Congress Cataloging-in-Publication Data

Inspectors general : overview, independence and effectiveness / editors, Anderson Lewis and Todd F. Hill.
p. cm.
Includes index.
CRS report for Congress prepared for members and committees of Congress.
ISBN 978-1-61942-205-6 (soft cover)
1. Finance, Public--Auditing--Law and legislation--United States. 2. Governmental investigations--United States. 3. Waste in government spending--Prevention--United States. 4. Executive departments--United States--Auditing. 5. Administrative agencies--United States--Auditing. I. Lewis, Anderson. II. Hill, Todd F.
KF6231.A56I57 2012
343.73'03--dc23

2011043450

Published by Nova Science Publishers, Inc. † New York

CONTENTS

PREFACE

There are more than 60 offices of inspectors general in executive and legislative branch agencies, as well as special inspectors general, who are responsible for audits and investigations related to particular programs or expenditures. Inspectors General draw their authorities and duties from the Inspector General Act of 1978. This book addresses the duties and functions of statutory Inspectors General (IGs); the numbers of each type of IG; the differences between IGs appointed by the President and those appointed by the agency head; considerations for whether certain IGs should be appointed by the President as opposed to the agency head; and the Inspector General Reform Act of 2008.

Chapter 1- This report addresses the duties and functions of statutory Inspectors General (IGs); the numbers of each type of IG; the differences between IGs appointed by the President and those appointed by the agency head; considerations for whether certain IGs should be appointed by the President as opposed to the agency head; and the Inspector General Reform Act of 2008 (Reform Act), P.L. 110-409. In October 2008, Congress enacted the Reform Act, which created additional protections and authorities for IGs with regard to removal or transfer of an IG, budgets, law enforcement authority, pay, subpoena power, and websites.

This report also addresses proposed changes affecting offices of inspectors general (OIGs) or establishing new OIGs in select bills in the 111th Congress: H.R. 885/S. 1354, the Improved Financial Commodity Markets Oversight and Accountability Act; H.R. 3126, the Consumer Financial Protection Agency Act of 2009; and H.R. 3962, the Affordable Health Care for America Act. On March 25, 2009, the House Committee on Oversight and Government Reform's Subcommittee on Government Management, Organization, and

Procurement held a hearing entitled, "The Roles and Responsibilities of Inspectors General within Financial Regulatory Agencies," at which the subcommittee discussed H.R. 885 and other issues. The House passed H.R. 885 on a voice vote under suspension of the rules on June 8, 2009.

Chapter 2- The Dodd-Frank Wall Street Reform and Consumer Protection Act (Dodd-Frank Act) required GAO to report on the relative independence, effectiveness, and expertise of the inspectors general (IG) established by the IG Act of 1978, as amended (IG Act), including IGs appointed by the President with Senate confirmation and those appointed by their agency heads in designated federal entities (DFE). GAO was also required to report on the effect that provisions in the Dodd-Frank Act have on IG independence.

The objectives of this report are to provide information as reported by the IGs on (1) the implementation of provisions intended to enhance their independence in the IG Reform Act of 2008 (Reform Act), the IG Act, and the Dodd-Frank Act; (2) their measures of effectiveness, including oversight of American Recovery and Reinvestment Act of 2009 (Recovery Act) funds; and (3) their expertise and qualifications in areas specified by the IG Act.

GAO relied primarily on responses to its survey received from 62 IGs established by the IG Act. GAO also obtained information from the President's fiscal year 2011 budget, the IGs' annual report to the President for fiscal year 2009, and the IGs' semiannual reports to the Congress.

GAO is not making any recommendations in this report. In comments on a draft of this report, the Council of the Inspectors General on Integrity and Efficiency (IG Council) stated the report contributes to a greater understanding of the work of the IGs in providing oversight to a wide range of government programs.

In: Inspectors General
Editors: A. Lewis and T. F. Hill

ISBN: 978-1-61942-205-6

Chapter 1

STATUTORY OFFICES OF INSPECTORS GENERAL: METHODS OF APPOINTMENT AND LEGISLATIVE PROPOSALS*

Vanessa K. Burrows

SUMMARY

This report addresses the duties and functions of statutory Inspectors General (IGs); the numbers of each type of IG; the differences between IGs appointed by the President and those appointed by the agency head; considerations for whether certain IGs should be appointed by the President as opposed to the agency head; and the Inspector General Reform Act of 2008 (Reform Act), P.L. 110-409. In October 2008, Congress enacted the Reform Act, which created additional protections and authorities for IGs with regard to removal or transfer of an IG, budgets, law enforcement authority, pay, subpoena power, and websites.

This report also addresses proposed changes affecting offices of inspectors general (OIGs) or establishing new OIGs in select bills in the 111th Congress: H.R. 885/S. 1354, the Improved Financial Commodity Markets Oversight and Accountability Act; H.R. 3126, the Consumer Financial Protection Agency Act of 2009; and H.R. 3962, the Affordable

---

* This is an edited, reformatted and augmented version of a Congressional Research Service publication, CRS Report for Congress R40675, from www.crs.gov, dated November 6, 2009.

Health Care for America Act. On March 25, 2009, the House Committee on Oversight and Government Reform's Subcommittee on Government Management, Organization, and Procurement held a hearing entitled, "The Roles and Responsibilities of Inspectors General within Financial Regulatory Agencies," at which the subcommittee discussed H.R. 885 and other issues. The House passed H.R. 885 on a voice vote under suspension of the rules on June 8, 2009.

OVERVIEW

There are more than 60 offices of inspectors general (OIGs) in executive and legislative branch agencies, as well as special inspectors general (SIGs), who are responsible for audits and investigations related to particular programs or expenditures. Inspectors General (IGs) draw their authorities and duties, either in whole or in part, from the Inspector General Act of 1978, as amended (IG Act).[1] For example, while several legislative branch IGs have been created in separate statutes, their establishing acts reference several of the provisions of the IG Act. Similarly, Congress has established SIGs such as the SIG for Iraq Reconstruction (SIGIR), the SIG for Afghanistan Reconstruction (SIGAR), and the SIG for the Troubled Asset Relief Program (SIGTARP), and has granted these IGs many of the authorities and responsibilities listed in the IG Act.

The IG Act addresses the authorities and duties of two types of IGs: (1) federal establishment IGs, who are appointed by the President with the advice and consent of the Senate and may be removed only by the President; and (2) designated federal entity (DFE) IGs,[2] who are appointed and may removed by the agency head.[3] The latter are typically found in the smaller agencies. IGs have been granted a substantial amount of independence, authority, and resources in their statutes to combat fraud, waste, and abuse. IGs operate under only the "general supervision" of the agency head, who is prohibited (with a few exceptions) from preventing or prohibiting an IG from carrying out an audit or investigation or issuing a subpoena.[4]

The statutory purposes of the OIGs include: conducting and supervising audits and investigations within an agency; providing policy recommendations for activities to promote the economy, efficiency, and effectiveness of agency programs and operations; and conducting, supervising, or coordinating activities designed to prevent and detect fraud and abuse in agency programs and operations.[5] IGs must also keep the agency head and Congress "fully and currently informed" about problems with the administration of agency programs and operations through specified reports and otherwise (which includes testifying at hearings and meeting with Members and staff).[6] The reports include semi-annual reports as well as immediate reports regarding "particularly serious or flagrant problems."[7] The connections between IGs and Congress may enhance legislative oversight capabilities and provide IGs with potential support for their findings and recommendations for corrective action.

To carry out these and other duties, IGs have access to agency information and subpoena power for records and documents, as well as independent law enforcement authority. IGs must report suspected violations of federal criminal law immediately to the Attorney General.[8] Agencies may also have a separate office that is responsible for conducting criminal investigations under the statutes that the agency is responsible for administering and enforcing, which may make recommendations for further investigation and prosecution to the U.S. Department of Justice.

TYPES OF IGS

Including the newest IG for the Federal Housing Finance Agency, there are presently 30 establishment IGs that have been appointed by the President. They are located in the following departments and agencies: (1) Agriculture; (2) Commerce; (3) Defense; (4) Education; (5) Energy; (6) Health and Human Services; (7) Housing and Urban Development; (8) Interior; (9) Justice; (10) Labor; (11) State; (12) Transportation; (13) Homeland Security; (14) Treasury; (15) Veterans Affairs; (16) Environmental Protection Agency; (17) General Services Administration; (18) National Aeronautics and Space Administration; (19) Nuclear Regulatory Commission; (20) Office of Personnel Management; (21) Railroad Retirement Board; (22) Federal Deposit Insurance Corporation; (23) Small Business Administration; (24) Corporation for National and Community Service; (25) Agency for International Development; (26) Social Security Administration; (27) Federal Housing Finance Agency; (28) Tennessee Valley Authority; (29) Export-Import Bank; and (30) Treasury Inspector General for Tax Administration.[9] The IG Act also provides that IGs may be established in commissions created under 40 U.S.C. § 15301, which are the Southeast Crescent Regional Commission, the Southwest Border Regional Commission, and the Northern Border Regional Commission.

Not including the IG for the Federal Housing Finance Board, as that agency has become part of the new Federal Housing Finance Agency, there are currently 29 DFE IGs, appointed by the agency head and located in the following agencies: (1) Amtrak; (2) Appalachian Regional Commission; (3) Board of Governors of the Federal Reserve System; (4) Commodity Futures Trading Commission; (5) Consumer Product Safety Commission; (6) Corporation for Public Broadcasting; (7) Denali Commission; (8) Equal Employment Opportunity Commission; (9) Farm Credit Administration; (10) Federal Communications Commission; (11) Federal Election Commission; (12) Election Assistance Commission; (13) Federal Maritime Commission; (14) Federal Labor Relations Authority; (15) Federal Trade Commission; (16) Legal Services Corporation; (17) National Archives and Records Administration; (18) National Credit Union Administration; (19) National Endowment for the Arts; (20) National Endowment for the Humanities; (21) National Labor Relations Board; (22) National Science Foundation; (23) Peace Corps; (24) Pension Benefit Guaranty Corporation; (25) Securities and Exchange Commission; (26) Smithsonian Institution; (27) United States International Trade Commission; (28) Postal Regulatory Commission; and (29) United States Postal Service.[10]

There are several additional types of IGs that draw their authorities in part from the IG Act. The five legislative branch IGs are located in the following entities: (1) Government Accountability Office; (2) Architect of the Capitol; (3) Government Printing Office; (4) Library of Congress; and (5) Capitol Police. There are three Special IGs: (1) SIGIR, (2) SIGAR, and (3) SIGTARP. Finally, there is an IG for the Central Intelligence Agency (CIA) and an IG for the Office of the Director of National Intelligence (ODNI).

Differences Between Establishment and DFE IGs

The IG Act of 1978 created IGs in a small number of executive branch agencies known as establishments.[11] The IG Act Amendments of 1988 expanded the number of presidentially-appointed establishment IGs and also created DFE IGs.[12] The House Report on an earlier version of the 1988 amendments stated that although most of the DFEs at the time had "audit units and some also have investigative units ... the extension of the 1978 act is necessary, because many of these entities have failed to comply with longstanding requirements regarding independence" of such units.[13]

The most notable difference between establishment IGs and DFE IGs is the individual who appoints and who may remove or transfer the IG—for establishment IGs, this individual is the President and for DFE IGs, this person is the agency head. Another key difference between establishment and DFE

IGs is that establishment IGs receive a separate appropriations account or a line item in the establishment's appropriations.[14] In contrast, each DFE IG's budget is part of the parent entity's budget process.[15] A 1992 guidance memorandum from the Office of Management and Budget (OMB) stated that "because of the reporting relationship established by the IG Act, entity heads must make entity budget formulation and budget execution decisions affecting the IG."[16] OMB stated that it was "expected that entity heads will apply agency budget reductions, redistributions, sequestrations, or pay raise absorptions to the Office of the IG with due consideration to the effect that such application would have on the Office's ability to carry out its statutory responsibilities."[17] OMB's guidance added that the IG was to "have an ongoing dialogue with the OMB budget examiner" regarding the IG's "operational plans, activities, and accomplishments."[18] The Reform Act created additional safeguards for IG budgets. Section 8 of the Reform Act addressed the reporting of the IG's initial budget estimate to the head of the establishment or DFE. The budget estimate includes the budget request, a request for funds for training, and amounts necessary to support the newly created Council of the Inspectors General on Integrity and Efficiency (CIGIE). The establishment or DFE head must then include this information, as well as comments of the IG, when transmitting the request to the President. The President, in turn, must then include in his budget submission: the IG's budget estimate; the President's requested amounts for the IG, IG training, and support of the CIGIE; and comments of the affected IG, if the IG determines that the President's budget would "substantially inhibit" the IG from performing his or her duties.

Other less apparent differences also exist between establishment IGs and DFE IGs, such as how the two types of IGs may be selected and how they may select their own employees. The DFE IGs are exempt from the sections of the IG Act (§§ 6(a)(7) and (a)(8)) that mandate the selection, appointment, and employment of officers and employees in establishment IG offices according to civil service employment laws. The House Report on a version of the 1988 IG Act amendments stated that "the committee recognizes that not all Federal entities operate under the Civil Service personnel system," and therefore Congress did not extend such provisions regarding employee hiring to DFE IGs.[19] DFEs have been exempt from these requirements for establishment OIGs since DFEs were created. DFE IGs must be appointed by the head of the agency "in accordance with the applicable laws and regulations governing appointments within" the agency.[20] The DFE IGs, in turn, must hire employees for their offices "subject to the applicable laws and regulation that govern such selections, appointments, and employment, and the obtaining of such services, within the [DFE]."[21]

Another difference relates to the use of legal counsel by IGs. The different relationships between establishment and DFE IGs and their attorneys were delineated in the Reform Act. The act specified that an establishment IG must receive legal advice from an attorney who is hired under civil service laws and reports directly to the IG or to another IG. The Reform Act also provided three ways for a DFE to obtain counsel. First, a DFE IG could obtain counsel from an attorney appointed by the IG (according to the DFE-specific laws and regulations governing appointments within the DFE) who reports directly to the IG. Second, DFE IGs, on a reimbursable basis, could obtain services from a counsel who is appointed by and who reports to another IG. Third, the DFE IG may obtain the legal services of an appropriate person on the CIGIE.[22]

The Reform Act continued preexisting differences between the two types of IGs addressed in the IG Act. For example, the Reform Act increased the pay of establishment IGs, the CIA IG, SIGIR, and SIGAR to the rate of level III of the Executive Schedule, plus 3%.[23] The Reform Act increased the pay of DFE IGs as well, but did not link them to the Executive Schedule. The Reform Act provided that DFE IGs should be classified for pay purposes at a level at or above a majority of the senior level executives of the DFE (such as a General Counsel or Chief Acquisition Officer), but that the pay could not be less than the average total compensation, including bonuses, of those senior level executives.[24] The Reform Act also provided that a DFE IG's pay could not increase by more than 25% of the DFE IG's average total pay for the previous three fiscal years.[25]

Prior to the Reform Act, additional disparities existed between establishment and DFE IGs. That act required DFE IGs, like their establishment IG counterparts, to be appointed based only on the individual's skills in auditing or other relevant areas.[26] In the conference report for the Inspector General Act Amendments of 1988, the conferees indicated that they "intend that the head of the designated Federal entity appoint the Inspector General without regard to political affiliation and solely on the basis of integrity and demonstrated ability in accounting, auditing, financial analysis, law, management analysis, public administration, or investigations."[27] However, this sentiment was not added to the law until the Reform Act was enacted. Additionally, the Reform Act provided that the CIGIE must submit recommendations for nominees to establishment, DFE, CIA, and ODNI IG positions.[28]

The Reform Act also granted law enforcement authority to DFE IGs, which was previously only available to establishment IGs, including the authority to carry firearms, make arrests without warrants, and seek and execute arrest warrants.[29]

Additionally, the Reform Act addressed a protection that DFE IGs enjoyed that was not previously available for establishment IGs—the Reform Act added a provision regarding transfers of establishment IGs to the clause regarding how the establishment IGs may be removed by the President. The removal clause for DFE IGs previously mentioned transfers of DFE IGs, but did not provide the notification requirement added by the Reform Act. As mentioned previously, the Reform Act provided that the President and the agency head must notify Congress of the reasons for a removal or transfer of an IG in writing at least 30 days before removing or transferring the IG.[30] Previously, the DFE heads had to notify Congress in writing when removing an IG, while the President was not required to communicate the reasons for removal to Congress in writing.

LEGISLATION

This section will discuss proposed changes affecting offices of inspectors general (OIGs) or establishing new OIGs in select bills in the 111th Congress: H.R. 885/S. 1354, the Improved Financial Commodity Markets Oversight and Accountability Act; H.R. 3126, the Consumer Financial Protection Agency Act of 2009; and H.R. 3962, the Affordable Health Care for America Act.

H.R. 885/S. 1354: Improved Financial Commodity Markets Oversight and Accountability Act

On June 6, 2009, the House passed H.R. 885, which would elevate five DFE IGs in entities that address financial issues—the IGs for the Board of Governors of the Federal Reserve System; the Commodity Futures Trading Commission (CFTC); the National Credit Union Administration (NCUA); the Pension Benefit Guaranty Corporation (PBGC); and the Securities and Exchange Commission (SEC)—to the status of presidentially-appointed, Senate-confirmed IGs. The changes would take effect 30 days after the law is enacted. The IGs that currently serve as the head of the OIG offices in those DFEs could continue serving as the IGs until the President makes an appointment under the IG Act procedures. Nothing in H.R. 885 would prohibit the President from appointing the individuals currently serving as the DFE IGs to the new presidentially-appointed IG positions.

Initially, H.R. 885 provided that IGs acting in that capacity would remain subject to current DFE limitations, such as those on authorities and pay. However, as amended, H.R. 885 "ensures that the changes made by the legislation do not interfere with existing pay structures ... as they relate to the position of inspector general and other employees."[31]

Other amendments to H.R. 885, as passed by the House, included provisions relating to the continuation of personnel. As mentioned above, these five DFE IGs are exempt from the sections of the IG Act (§§ 6(a)(7) and (a)(8)) that mandate the selection, appointment, and employment of officers and employees in establishment IG offices according to civil service employment laws. H.R. 885 would preserve that distinction for these five IGs, though they would be elevated to presidentially-appointed IGs.[32]

H.R. 885 would change the authorities of the five DFE IGs in the bill in a significant way with respect to other establishment and DFE IGs, as H.R. 885 would grant these IGs the ability to subpoena testimony as well as documents.[33] Under H.R. 885, the five DFE IGs would be able to subpoena testimony not just of agency employees, but also of contractors, grantees, and persons or entities regulated by the establishment.[34] Presently, § 6(a)(4) of the IG Act provides IGs with the authority to subpoena "documentary evidence necessary in the performance of the functions assigned by this Act." Subpoena authority under the IG Act is delegable,[35] and subpoenas issued under the act are judicially enforceable.[36] The IG Act contains no explicit prohibition on disclosure of the existence or specifics of a subpoena issued under this authority.

Finally, H.R. 885 would create a new provision regarding the responses of establishment agency heads to reports by these five IGs. A similar provision was included with respect to reports issued by the SIGTARP in § 4 of P.L. 111-15, the Special Inspector General for the Troubled Asset Relief Program Act of 2009, which was passed by Congress earlier this year. Under H.R. 885, the heads of these five establishments must either "take action to address deficiencies identified by a report or investigation" of the establishment's IG or "certify to both Houses of Congress that no action is necessary or appropriate in connection with" such a deficiency.[37]

H.R. 3126: Consumer Financial Protection Agency Act of 2009

Sections 115(a)(3) and 181 of the discussion draft of H.R. 3126 appear to create a DFE IG for the proposed Consumer Financial Protection Agency (CFPA).[38] Section 115(a) of the discussion draft states that the Director of the CFPA shall appoint the CFPA IG, who shall have the authority and functions of a DFE IG .[39] Section 181 of the discussion draft would amend the IG Act to add the CFPA to the list of DFEs.[40]

H.R. 3962: Affordable Health Care for America Act

Section 1647 of H.R. 3962 would create a presidentially-appointed, Senate-confirmed establishment IG for the Health Choices Administration (HCA).[41] In addition to the authorities provided to establishment IGs in the IG Act, H.R. 3962 would grant the HCA IG the authority to conduct, supervise, and coordinate audits, evaluations, and investigations of the programs and operations of the HCA, including matters relating to fraud, abuse, and misconduct in connection with the admission and continued participation of any health benefits plan participating in the Health Insurance Exchange.[42] The IG also would have the authority to conduct audits, evaluations, and investigations relating to any private Health Insurance Exchange-participating health benefits plan. In consultation with the HHS IG, the IG for the HCA would have the authority to conduct audits, evaluations, and investigations relating to the public health insurance option. The IG would also have access to all relevant records, including records relating to claims paid by the health benefits plans that participate in the Health Insurance Exchange.

The authorities that would be granted to the HCA and the IG would not limit the duties, authorities, and responsibilities of the HHS IG, as in existence as of the date of enactment of the act, to oversee HHS programs and operations. The HHS IG would retain primary jurisdiction over fraud and abuse in connection with payments made under the public health insurance option.

Potential Considerations for Converting Certain DFE IGs to Presidentially-Appointed IGs

Elevating DFE IGs, such as the five identified in H.R. 885, to presidentially-appointed, Senate-confirmed (PAS) positions would be within Congress's discretion, as provided for in the Constitution. Article II, section 2, clause 2 states that "the Congress may by Law vest the Appointment of such inferior Officers, as they think proper, in the President alone, in the Courts of Law, or in the Heads of Departments."[43] Many PAS positions other than high-level policy positions have been created because Congress saw a need to establish such position as one requiring advice and consent. This section discusses several potential considerations, which could be construed as advantages or disadvantages of establishing these five DFE IGs as PAS positions.[44] There are several approaches that Congress could pursue—(1) taking no action; (2) converting some DFE IGs into PAS positions; (3) converting all DFE IGs into PAS positions; or (4) converting some or all DFE IGs into PAS positions but including a sunset provision.[45] If a sunset provision were added to a statute converting some or all of the DFE IGs, Congress could then evaluate the benefits and drawbacks of granting PAS status to some or all of these IGs. The PAS positions could automatically revert to agency appointments after a period of time unless Congress made such changes permanent. CRS takes no position as to which of these options would be most desirable.

A conversion of some or all of these positions to PAS positions could have both positive and negative effects. Some of the advantages may be that the PAS process ensures that potential appointees are subject to more extensive ethical and political scrutiny, and IGs appointed under the PAS process may have greater credibility than their agency head appointed counterparts. Congress, specifically the Senate, may indirectly exert greater influence over the selection process and prevent unqualified individuals from being appointed. The prestige of a presidential appointment may also attract additional candidates. Some of the disadvantages of the PAS process may be that the politicization of the process could deter well-qualified candidates (although politicization may be less likely with IGs, due to their statutory qualifications regarding appointment without regard to political affiliation). Potential nominees may be required to submit a large quantity of paperwork as the President, and later the Senate, considers the individual's merits. As a result, the establishment of additional PAS positions may increase the workload of Senate committees and consume time and resources that could be used for other pending issues.

If an appointee is confirmed by the Senate, that IG may be seen as more credible and accountable to Congress than an appointee who does not require Senate confirmation. During the confirmation hearing, the Senate may obtain commitments from the IG appointee to respond to future requests for testimony. Such specific commitments with regard to future testimony may not be necessary, as the IG Act provides that the IGs have a duty to keep Congress "fully and currently informed."[46] However, such commitments may ease the process for obtaining IG testimony in the future. The Senate may also seek additional commitments during the confirmation process and explain its vision for the position or for the agency. At the same time, the PAS process may increase congressional involvement in the organization and activities of the DFE. Confirmation hearings for the IG could be used as a vehicle to conduct oversight of the DFE and its programs and operations. Additionally, the IG appointee may have developed relationships with Senators and congressional staff throughout the appointment process. However, the practical effect of these considerations may be limited as the IG Act indicates that DFE and establishment IGs are accountable to Congress, due, in part, to their reporting requirements.

Alternatively, it could be argued that maintaining the status quo for these IGs provides the President with greater flexibility in terms of managing staff, in that a typical conversion of a non-PAS position into a PAS position might make such IGs more amenable to indirect congressional control. Such amenability could undermine presidential control as compared to the status quo. The President could stand to lose, as IGs appointed by the agency heads alone may be more responsive and accountable to the President and more likely to implement his priorities, if any, for the IG office. Allegiance from DFE IGs under the current system arguably may assist the President's ability to address problems quickly. However, unlike other positions being considered for conversion to the level of a presidential appointment, IGs are perhaps unique because they are already accountable to Congress in terms of their statutory responsibilities, and they also have specified qualifications required for appointment. As a result, the potential loss of presidential power may not be as great with the conversion to a PAS position as it would otherwise seem to be due to a potential increase in indirect congressional control with the change to a PAS appointment, because Congress already retains and exerts control with regard to DFE IGs.

Because of the nature of the agencies being considered in H.R. 885, the President would only appear to retain more control over the appointment of the five DFE IGs under the status quo if he also gained more control over the agency boards. The Federal Reserve, CFTC, NCUA, and the SEC are independent agencies.[47] These independent agencies are insulated from complete Executive Branch control as they are headed by multi-member boards. For example, the boards of the CFTC, SEC, and NCUA are comprised of members of both political parties, but may have no more than a simple majority from one political party. In addition, the board membership at these agencies is determined according to staggered terms, so that not all of the members may be replaced at once. The Federal Reserve Board of Governors and the SEC Commissioners have for cause removal protection.[48] Therefore, arguably, the President may have more control over the five IGs if they are converted to PAS positions and the President is able to appoint those IGs himself. This would appear to be true even though the nominee would be approved through the advice and consent process.

Furthermore, DFE heads, who are politically aligned with the President, would likely prefer to maintain their influence on the selection process of the DFE's IG. Such appointment power may enable the DFE head to exercise greater control over the agency, posing questions of intrusion on the IG's independence. A DFE head's appointment power may help curry favor with the IG, as the DFE head is responsible for hiring and firing the IG. If the DFE IGs were converted to PAS positions, the agency head may still have some level of influence as the President may consult with the agency head when making an appointment to the IG position or when removing an IG.

Presidential appointees may also encounter procedural or political complications during the Senate confirmation process, such as a hold placed on a nomination. The confirmation process arguably provides the Senate with greater leverage during its negotiations with the Executive Branch over matters that may or may not be related to the appointment. Holds may be placed on nominations for various reasons. Whether as a result of a hold or other factors, the appointment process may be lengthy, thus potentially leading to longer vacancies.

The Government Accountability Office (GAO) has issued several reports dealing with IG structural and organizational changes. The reports considered the conversion of DFE IGs from agency head appointments and removals to presidential appointments and removals, which would affect the status and control of the current DFE IG offices. GAO concluded that such an arrangement would strengthen the independence, efficiency, and effectiveness of the DFE IG offices. In its 2002 report, GAO found no consensus among DFE and establishment IGs regarding the perceived impact of conversion.[49] The report noted that the presidentially-appointed IGs "generally indicated that DFE IG independence, quality, and use of resources could be strengthened by conversion," while the DFE IGs "indicated that there would be either no impact or that these elements could be weakened."[50] GAO called for dialogue among Congress, the IG community, and the affected agencies regarding specific conversions of DFE IGs.[51] In 2003, the Comptroller General similarly testified regarding GAO's determination that "if properly implemented, conversion ... and consolidation of IG offices could increase the overall independence, economy, efficiency, and effectiveness of IGs."[52] GAO testimony on March 25, 2009, similarly indicated that a change in the appointment of the IGs would result in a different level of independence.[53]

End Notes

[1] 5 U.S.C. Appendix.

[2] DFE IGs were created in the Inspector General Act Amendments of 1988, P.L. 100-504.

[3] Section 3 of the IG Reform Act of 2008 establishes a requirement that the President or the agency head must notify Congress in writing at least 30 days before removing or transferring an IG. P.L. 110-409. This report does not address potential constitutional concerns with this provision. Additionally, either an establishment or DFE IG may be impeached.

[4] 5 U.S.C. App. § 3(a).

[5] Although IGs oversee agency programs and operations, they do not have program operating responsibilities. *See* 5 U.S.C. App. §§ 8G(b), 9(a)(2); H.R. Rep. No. 100-1020, at 28 (Sept. 30, 1988) (Conf. Rept.).

[6] 5 U.S.C. App. §§ 2, 4(a)(5).

[7] 5 U.S.C. App. § 5(d)

[8] 5 U.S.C. App. § 4(d).

[9] Section 12(2) of Title 5 Appendix, United States Code, lists 32 IGs, including the IGs in numbers 1-29 in the above text. However, the IGs for the Federal Emergency Management Agency, the Community Development Financial Institutions Fund, and the Resolution Trust Corporation are no longer in existence. The functions of those agencies were either transferred or abolished. Also, 5 U.S.C. App. § 2 specifically lists the Office of Treasury IG for Tax Administration; the Treasury is defined as an establishment under 5 U.S.C. App. § 12(2).

[10] Section 8G(a)(2) of Title 5 Appendix, United States Code, lists several DFE IGs that are no longer in existence, have had their functions transferred, or are now presidentially-appointed IGs. For example, the FDIC IG is still listed in 5 U.S.C. § 8G(a)(2) as a DFE IG; however, he was made a presidentially-appointed IG. The Federal Housing Finance Board (FHFB) was merged into the Federal Housing Finance Agency (FHFA); the FHFA IG was added as an establishment IG on July 30, 2008, in P.L. 110-289, and does not

presently have a presidentially-appointed IG. The IG for the FHFB is serving as the Associate Director for Internal Audit, and he reports to the Office of the Director. The FHFA website states: "Until FHFA has an [OIG], employees or others who wish to report a violation of any law, rule or regulation, gross mismanagement, a gross waste of funds, an abuse of authority, or substantial and specific danger to public safety or complaints regarding the programs and operations of the agency may make a report or complaint to FHFA's Office of Internal Audit." FHFA, Office of Inspector General, http://www.fhfa.gov/Default.aspx?Page=122. The Panama Canal Commission ended with the transfer of the canal to Panama (22 U.S.C. § 3611). In P.L. 103-236, the Board for International Broadcasting was abolished and its functions were transferred to the U.S. Information Agency, of which the newly created Broadcasting Board of Governors (BBG) was a part. Currently, the Department of State IG is also the IG for the BBG. *See* 22 U.S.C. § 6203; Department of State, Office of Inspector General, http://oig.state.gov/. However, a January 2009 *Federal Register* notice listed the BBG IG as a separate DFE. 74 Fed. Reg. 3656 (Jan. 21, 2009).

[11] The initial establishments listed in P.L. 95-452 were the Departments of Agriculture, Commerce, Housing and Urban Development, Interior, Labor, and Transportation, as well as the Community Services Administration, the Environmental Protection Agency, the General Services Administration, the National Aeronautics and Space Administration, the Small Business Administration, and the Veterans' Administration. The IGs in these agencies followed the establishment of predecessors in 1976, in what is now the Department of Health and Human Services, and in 1977 in the Department of Energy.

[12] Initially, the DFEs in which the 1988 amendments created IGs were entities that were "(1) regulatory agencies of the Federal Government or (2) were established by the Federal Government and receive[d] over $100 million annually in Federal funds." H.R. Rep. No. 100-771, Inspector General Act Amendments of 1988, at 2 (July 13, 1988).

[13] *Id.* at 13.

[14] 31 U.S.C. § 1105(a)(25).

[15] This appropriations information for designated federal entity OIG appropriations is derived from a May 27, 2008 memorandum by Frederick M. Kaiser, Specialist in National Government, CRS. For coverage of this and other matters, see also GAO, *Designated Federal Entities: Survey of Governance Practices and the Inspector General Role*, GAO009-270 (April 2009), http://www.gao.gov/new.items/d09270.pdf.

[16] Memorandum from Frank Hodsoll, Office of Management and Budget, *Inspectors General in Designated Federal Entities: Key Statutory Provisions and Implementing Guidance* (Nov. 13, 1992), at 6.

[17] *Id.* at 7.

[18] *Id.*

[19] H.R. Rep. No. 100-771, Inspector General Act Amendments of 1988, at 16 (July 13, 1988).

[20] 5 U.S.C. App. § 8G(c).

[21] 5 U.S.C. App. § 8G(g)(2).

[22] P.L. 110-409, § 6; 5 U.S.C. App. § 8G(g)(4).

[23] 5 U.S.C. § 5314.

[24] P.L. 110-409, § 4(b). As a result, some DFE IGs may make more than their establishment IG counterparts.

[25] Additionally, federal employees appointed to serve as IGs could not have their pay reduced as a result of being appointed to the IG position, nor could IGs currently serving have their pay reduced as a result of the law's enactment.

62, § 1647(b)(2).
d be noted that the President could be vested with authority to appoint IGs alone. For nple, SIGAR is a presidentially-appointed, but not Senate-confirmed, IG. 5 U.S.C. . § 8G note.
ction summarizes some concerns outlined in CRS Report RL32212, *The Appropriate ber of Advice and Consent Positions: An Analysis of the Issue and Proposals for nge*, by Henry B. Hogue (Mar. 14, 2005; out of print but available from author).
eparate approach, legislation could also consolidate an IG office in a DFE under the ce of an IG in an establishment, as Congress accomplished with the oversight of the adcasting Board of Governors by the Department of State IG.
C. App. §§ 2, 4(a)(5).
GC is a federal corporation.
.C. § 242; *SEC v. Blinder, Robinson & Co.*, 855 F.2d 677, 681 (10th Cir. 1988).
Inspectors General: Office Consolidation and Related Issues, GAO-02-575 (2002).
.
.
ent of David M. Walker, Comptroller General, GAO, *Inspectors General: Enhancing eral Accountability*, GAO-04-117T (2003), at 1.
ep. No. 111-114, at 4 (May 18, 2009).

[26] P.L. 110-409, § 2.

[27] H.R. Rep. No. 100-1020, at 27 (Sept. 30, 1988) (Conf. Rep

[28] P.L. 110-409, § 7(c)(1)(F).

[29] P.L. 110-409, § 11.

[30] P.L. 110-409, § 3.

[31] H.R. Rep. No. 111-114, at 3-4 (May 18, 2009).

[32] H.R. 885, § 3 (adding § 8M to the IG Act).

[33] In *National Aeronautics and Space Administration* (NA Supreme Court remarked on this limitation of the IG A the authority to subpoena documents and information, t 242 (1999); *see also* United States v. Iannone, 610 F.2d 9

[34] H.R. 885, § 4. IGs would have the ability "to require, b employee of a contractor or grantee of the establishme subcontractor or subgrantee of such a contractor or g regulated by the establishment, any records and testimo of functions assigned" to the IG. *Id.*

[35] *United States v. Custodian of Records*, 743 F. Supp. 783, 7 *U.S. Postal Service*, 771 F. Supp. 138, 140 (E.D. Va. 199

[36] 5 U.S.C. App. § 6(a)(4)("... which subpena, in the case of co be enforceable by order of any appropriate United State *General v. Banner Plumbing Supply Co., Inc.*, 34 F. S *University of Medicine and Dentistry v. Corrigan*, 347 F.3

[37] H.R. 885, § 5.

[38] This section examines the powers of the CFPA as set September 25th discussion draft of the Consumer Finar 2009, http://financialservices.house.gov/Key_Issues/Financial_R gulatoryReform/Discussion_Drafts/Discussion_Draft_of_([hereinafter Discussion Draft]. The House Committee on l draft (which was ordered to be reported, as amended amendments on Oct. 22, 2009, but a version of the discuss is not publicly available as of the date of this report. The and Commerce approved the bill, which was ordered to be 29, 2009.

[39] Section 115(a) of the discussion draft refers to the IG having an inspector general of a designated federal entity under 1978 (*5 U.S.C. App. 3*)." (emphasis added) It appears that 3, which concerns the appointment and removal of presider IGs, may be intended to serve as the reference for all of th just § 3 of the IG Act, as set forth in 5 U.S.C. Appendix. intended to be an establishment IG, or a DFE IG appoint with the authority and functions of an IG under 5 U.S.C. A and 181 of the discussion draft would likely need to be rewo

[40] Section 181 of the discussion draft again refers to 5 U establishment IG section.

[41] This section would add the HCA to the list of establishments i add the Commissioner of the HCA to the list of establish 3962, § 1647(b)(1).

[42] H.R. 3

[43] It sho ex Ap

[44] This s Nu Ch

[45] As a of Br

[46] 5 U.S

[47] The F

[48] 12 U.

[49] GAO

[50] *Id.* at

[51] *Id.* at

[52] State Fe

[53] H.R.

In: Inspectors General
Editors: A. Lewis and T. F. Hill
ISBN: 978-1-61942-205-6

Chapter 2

INSPECTORS GENERAL REPORTING ON INDEPENDENCE, EFFECTIVENESS, AND EXPERTISE*

The United States Government Accountability Office

ABBREVIATIONS:

IG	statutory federal inspector general
IG Act	Inspector General Act of 1978, as amended
IG Council	Council of the Inspectors General on Integrity and Efficiency
DFE	designated federal entity
Dodd-Frank Act	Dodd-Frank Wall Street Reform and Consumer Protection Act
Recovery Act	American Recovery and Reinvestment Act of 2009
Recovery Board	Recovery Accountability and Transparency Board
Reform Act	IG Reform Act of 2008

* This is an edited, reformatted and augmented version of the The United States Government Accountability Office publication, Report to Congressional Committees GAO-11-770, dated September 2011.

WHY GAO DID THIS STUDY

The Dodd-Frank Wall Street Reform and Consumer Protection Act (Dodd-Frank Act) required GAO to report on the relative independence, effectiveness, and expertise of the inspectors general (IG) established by the IG Act of 1978, as amended (IG Act), including IGs appointed by the President with Senate confirmation and those appointed by their agency heads in designated federal entities (DFE). GAO was also required to report on the effect that provisions in the Dodd-Frank Act have on IG independence.

The objectives of this report are to provide information as reported by the IGs on (1) the implementation of provisions intended to enhance their independence in the IG Reform Act of 2008 (Reform Act), the IG Act, and the Dodd-Frank Act; (2) their measures of effectiveness, including oversight of American Recovery and Reinvestment Act of 2009 (Recovery Act) funds; and (3) their expertise and qualifications in areas specified by the IG Act.

GAO relied primarily on responses to its survey received from 62 IGs established by the IG Act. GAO also obtained information from the President's fiscal year 2011 budget, the IGs' annual report to the President for fiscal year 2009, and the IGs' semiannual reports to the Congress.

GAO is not making any recommendations in this report. In comments on a draft of this report, the Council of the Inspectors General on Integrity and Efficiency (IG Council) stated the report contributes to a greater understanding of the work of the IGs in providing oversight to a wide range of government programs.

WHAT GAO FOUND

Information from the 62 IGs in offices established by the IG Act and GAO's analysis showed that the IGs had (1) taken actions to implement statutory provisions intended to enhance their independence; (2) reported billions of dollars in potential savings and other measures of effectiveness, including actions taken to help prevent fraud in the distribution of Recovery Act funds; and (3) a range of expertise and qualifications in the areas specified by the IG Act.

With respect to independence, the IGs reported that

- statutory provisions regarding IG compensation have been implemented where applicable, thereby maintaining the independence of their work and enhancing their relative stature within their agencies;
- they had access to independent legal counsel who reports to an IG instead of an agency management official;
- only one IG used a statutory provision for IGs to report particularly flagrant problems through the agency head to the Congress in 7 days because issues are generally resolved before the report is needed; and
- of the affected 26 DFE IGs, 14 responded that their independence was enhanced by the Dodd-Frank Act provision that changed the designation of agency head from the chair to the entire board or commission, and 20 responded that their independence was enhanced by the provision requiring a two-thirds majority vote for IG removal.

Also, the IGs' budgets were not always identified separately in the President's fiscal year 2011 budget submission as required by the Reform Act provision intended to enhance the IGs' budget independence through transparent reporting. The IG Council is currently reviewing the matter.

The IGs reported various measures of effectiveness. The IGs reported potential savings of about $43.3 billion resulting from their fiscal year 2009 audits and investigations. Given the IGs' fiscal year 2009 budget authority of about $2.3 billion, these potential savings represent about an $18 return on every dollar invested in the IGs. The IGs also reported about 5,900 criminal actions, 1,100 civil actions, 4,400 suspensions and debarments, and 6,100 indictments as a result of their work. In addition, the IGs reported enhanced effectiveness through additional actions taken to help prevent fraud in their agencies. For example, in fiscal year 2009 the Recovery Act created a requirement for the IGs to provide oversight of the economic stimulus funds disbursed by their agencies, and established the Recovery Accountability and Transparency Board of IG members to help carry out this oversight. As of June 2011, the IGs reported over 1,500 investigations opened, over 1,400 reviews completed, and over 2,000 training sessions provided to detect and prevent fraud, waste, abuse, and mismanagement in the use of Recovery Act funds.

With respect to expertise, the IGs reported having backgrounds, academic degrees, and certifications in a range of areas related to their statutory responsibilities. The IGs reported backgrounds and academic degrees in accounting, auditing, financial analysis, law, management analysis, public administration, and investigations. In addition, the IGs, particularly the DFE IGs, reported numerous professional certifications related to their responsibilities.

September 21, 2011
Congressional Committees

The statutory federal inspectors general (IG) are instrumental in enhancing government accountability through the results of independent audits, investigations, and other reports on federal government programs and operations. Independence is one of the most important elements of a strong performing IG function, helping to ensure that the IGs' work is viewed as impartial by both their agencies and the Congress. In addition, IGs must be independent in order to effectively carry out their mission to help prevent and detect fraud, waste, abuse, and mismanagement and promote economy, efficiency, and effectiveness. Further, to lead these efforts, the IGs must bring the necessary expertise to bear on their work through experience and professional qualifications.

As part of the Dodd-Frank Wall Street Reform and Consumer Protection Act (Dodd-Frank Act),[1] the Congress required GAO to report on the relative independence, effectiveness, and expertise of federal IGs appointed by the President and confirmed by the Senate (presidential) and those appointed by agency heads in designated federal agencies (DFE) as defined by the Inspector General Act of 1978, as amended (IG Act).[2] The Dodd-Frank Act also calls for GAO to report on the effect that provisions in the Dodd-Frank Act have on the independence of the IGs. Accordingly, the specific objectives of this report are to provide information as reported by the IGs on their relative (1) independence including the effect of provisions in the Dodd-Frank Act, (2) measures of effectiveness, and (3) expertise and qualifications.

BACKGROUND

The IG Act created independent IG offices at 30 major departments and agencies with IGs appointed by the President, confirmed by the Senate, and who may be removed only by the President with advance notice to the Congress stating the reasons. (A listing of these 30 departments and agencies with presidential IG offices is provided in app. I.) In 1988, the IG Act was amended to establish additional IG offices located in 33 DFEs defined by the act.[3] (A listing of the DFEs with IGs is provided in app. II.) Generally, the DFE IGs have the same authorities and responsibilities as those IGs originally established by the IG Act, but with the distinction that they are appointed and may be removed by their agency heads rather than by the President and are not subject to Senate confirmation. Although not in the scope of our review, there are 10 IGs established by other statutes with provisions similar to those in the IG Act. (A listing of the IGs established under other statutes is provided in app. III.)

The IGs appointed by the President are generally located in the largest departments and agencies of the government; the DFEs have smaller budgets and their IGs have correspondingly smaller budgets and fewer staff. The presidentially appointed IGs and the DFE IGs reported to us total budget authority for fiscal year 2010 of about $2.2 billion with approximately 13,652 authorized full-time equivalent staff and 13,390 staff on board at the end of fiscal year 2010. The presidentially appointed IGs' budget authority constituted about 84 percent (about $1.8 billion) of the total, and they had about 86 percent (11,564) of the total staff on board. The budgets of the DFE IGs made up about 16 percent (about $352 million) of the total budget authority for IGs, and they had about 14 percent (1,826) of the total staff on board at the end of fiscal year 2010.

The IG Reform Act of 2008 (Reform Act) amended the IG Act by adding requirements related to IG independence and effectiveness.[4] Among other provisions, the Reform Act requires the rate of basic pay of the IGs appointed by the President to be at a specified level, and for the DFE IGs, at or above a majority of other senior-level executives at their entities. The Reform Act also requires an IG to obtain legal advice from his or her own counsel or to obtain counsel from another IG's office or from the Council of the Inspectors General on Integrity and Efficiency (IG Council).[5] The IG Act also provides protections to the independence of the IGs while keeping both their agency heads and the Congress fully and currently informed about particularly flagrant problems and deficiencies within their agencies through a 7-day process specified by the act.

In addition, the Dodd-Frank Act amended the IG Act with provisions to enhance the independence of IGs in DFEs with boards or commissions. Specifically, the Dodd-Frank Act changed who would be considered the head of the DFE for purposes of IG appointment, general supervision, and reporting under the IG Act. If the DFE has a board or commission the amendments would now require each of these IGs to report organizationally to the entire board or commission as the head of the DFE rather than an individual chairman. In addition, the Dodd-Frank Act requires the written concurrence of a two-thirds majority of the board or commission to remove an IG. Prior to this protection, most DFE IGs reported to, and were subject to removal by, the individual serving as head of the DFE.

The Reform Act also included a provision intended to provide additional IG independence through the transparent reporting of their budgets. Specifically, the Reform Act requires the President's budget submission to the Congress to have the IGs' requested budget amounts identified separately within their respective agency budgets, along with any comments provided by the IGs on the sufficiency of their budgets.

The American Recovery and Reinvestment Act of 2009 (Recovery Act) is one of the federal government's key efforts to stimulate the economy in response to the most serious economic crisis since the Great Depression.[6] The Recovery Act provided for IG oversight of the funds by creating the Recovery Accountability and Transparency Board (Recovery Board), which has an IG Chairman and 12 additional IG board members to prevent and detect fraud, waste, and abuse in the stimulus-funded programs. Altogether, there are 30 IGs involved with the oversight of Recovery Act funds. (A listing of the IGs providing oversight of Recovery Act funds is provided in app. IV).

Also, the IG Act includes a provision addressing the qualifications and expertise of the IGs by specifying that each IG appointment is to be without regard to political affiliation and solely on the basis of integrity and demonstrated ability in accounting, auditing, financial analysis, law, management analysis, public administration, or investigation. The fields in which an IG can have experience are intended to be sufficiently diverse so that many qualified people could be considered, but also limited to areas relevant to the tasks considered necessary.[7] The IG Act Amendments of 1988 created DFE IGs but did not specify that these IG appointments made by agency heads were to be without regard to political affiliation and on the basis of demonstrated ability in specified fields. The Reform Act addressed the differences in criteria for IG appointment by providing the same provisions for both the DFE IGs and the IGs appointed by the President.

Scope and Methodology

We addressed our reporting objectives through our summary of responses to a survey sent to the federal statutory IGs established by the IG Act regarding their activities for fiscal year 2010, and additional analysis. We obtained and analyzed survey responses from 62 IGs established by the IG Act: including 30 IGs who were appointed by the President and confirmed by the Senate, and 32 DFE IGs.[8] We augmented the survey data with information obtained from prior GAO reports, the President's budget submission to the Congress for fiscal year 2011, and the IGs' semiannual reports to the C ongress.

For our discussion of the independence of the IGs, we summarized information from the responses to our survey questions about the implementation of selected provisions in the Reform Act, the IG Act, and the Dodd-Frank Act that are intended to enhance IG independence. Specifically, we asked all of the 62 IGs about the implementation of Reform Act provisions intended to keep IG pay and salaries at a specified level for IGs appointed by the President and consistent with other senior-level executives for the DFE IGs, and about the IGs' sources of legal counsel. Our survey also obtained information about the extent to which the IGs found it necessary to communicate particularly flagrant problems to their agency heads and the Congress within 7 days as prescribed by the IG Act. These IG reports are commonly referred to as 7-day letters.

Regarding the effect of Dodd-Frank Act provisions to enhance independence, we obtained the views of the 26 DFE IGs with boards or commissions on whether their independence was enhanced by these provisions designating their boards and commissions as DFE heads rather than individual chairmen, and the requirement for the concurrence of a two-thirds majority of the board or commission for removal of an IG. We also obtained information from the President's budget submission to the Congress for fiscal year 2011, to determine whether the IG budget amounts were separately identified along with any comments by the IGs regarding the sufficiency of their budgets.

To address the effectiveness of the IGs, we obtained information on the accomplishments of the IGs as reported to the IG Council for fiscal year 2009, in preparation for their annual report to the President.[9] We also obtained information reported by the Recovery Board on its mission and accomplishments in providing oversight of Recovery Act funds. In addition, our survey questionnaire obtained information for fiscal year 2010 on management challenges identified by the IGs reporting under requirements of the Reports Consolidation Act of 2000.[10] To identify the extent of oversight provided by the IGs, we summarized the reported management challenges to identify the major focus of these issues and obtained IG reports relevant to these issues provided by the IGs to our survey and from our review of the IGs' semiannual reports to the Congress.

To address the IGs' qualifications and expertise we summarized the 62 IGs' survey information provided on the background of each IG, including professional experience, academic degrees, and professional certifications obtained prior to being appointed to an IG position. We compared this information to the areas of demonstrated ability specified by the IG Act and summarized the number of IGs in each area.

We conducted our work from November 2010 to September 2011 in accordance with all sections of GAO's Quality Assurance Framework that are relevant to our objectives. The framework requires that we plan and perform the engagement to obtain sufficient and appropriate evidence to meet our stated objectives and to discuss any limitations in our work. We believe that the information and data obtained, and the analysis conducted, provide a reasonable basis for any findings and conclusions.

We requested comments on a draft of this report from the IG Council. Written comments from the IG Council are reprinted in appendix V and summarized in the "Agency Comments" section of this report. We also received and incorporated as appropriate technical comments from several IG offices.

INDEPENDENCE

Our survey obtained information from 62 federal IGs appointed under the IG Act on actions taken concerning legislative provisions in the Reform Act and the IG Act intended to enhance IG independence. The IGs reported

- pay that was at the specified levels required by the Reform Act for IGs appointed by the President and consistent with those of other senior-level officials as required for DFE IGs, thus helping to maintain IG independence and enhance their relative stature within their agencies by increasing their fixed compensation and eliminating discretionary compensation that could create a conflict of interest;
- having access to independent legal counsel reporting to an IG instead of an agency management official, thus helping to ensure the independence of legal advice available to the IG; and
- rarely using 7-day letters as a way to independently inform agency heads and the Congress of serious problems concerning agency operations because such issues were resolved without the need for such a letter.

We also surveyed the 26 DFE IGs affected by the Dodd-Frank Act provisions intended to enhance IG independence for those IGs reporting to boards or commissions.[11] Just over half of these IGs responded that the change of agency head to the full board or commission increased their independence and most responded that the requirements for a two-thirds concurrence among the board or commission members prior to an IG's removal increased their independence.

In addition, based on our review of the President's fiscal year 2011 budget submission to the Congress, the IGs' budget amounts were not always separately identified as required by the Reform Act. To the extent the IGs' budgets are separately identified, the added transparency of these amounts to the Congress can help increase IG independence. After we informed the IG Council about the results of our review concerning the IGs' budgets, they agreed to review and assess the matter.

IGs Reported Having Pay at Required Levels

The Reform Act addressed the compensation of IGs and requires that IGs appointed by the President have their pay adjusted from Executive Schedule IV to Executive Schedule III plus 3 percent. In addition, the Reform Act requires that the grade, level, or rank designation for the DFE IGs be set at or above that of a majority of the senior-level executives of the agency, such as the general counsel, chief acquisition officer, chief information officer, chief financial officer, and the chief human capital officer at that agency. In addition, the DFE IG pay cannot be less than the average total compensation (including bonuses) of the senior-level executives at that agency calculated on an annual basis.

Of the 30 IGs appointed by the President, 27 reported being at or even above the required pay level; with the remaining 3 IGs reporting that they were in acting positions and the requirement was not currently applicable to them. Of the 32 DFE IGs who responded to our survey, 29 reported that their pay and salaries were consistent with those of the senior-level executives of their agencies. Of the remaining 3 DFE IGs, 1 was newly established in fiscal year 2011 and had not yet determined an amount of pay consistent with senior-level executives, 1 IG reported having the correct salary but not the corresponding grade level, and 1 IG was in an acting capacity and reported the requirement was not currently applicable.

IGs Reported Having Access to Independent Legal Counsel

The Reform Act also requires that each IG established by the IG Act have his or her own legal counsel or obtain necessary legal counsel from another IG office or from the IG Council. In a March 1995 report, we reported that the IG community expressed concerns that IGs with attorneys located organizationally in their agencies' offices of general counsel would not always receive independent legal advice and that the IGs' own independence could be compromised.[12]

The results from our survey show that all the IGs established by the IG Act reported having access to a legal counsel that is organizationally independent, and none of the IGs rely on the general counsel offices of their agencies. For the 30 IGs appointed by the President, 29 employ their own legal counsel while 1 IG uses the legal services of another IG. All 32 DFE IGs who responded to our survey indicated that they obtain independent legal counsel, with 26 employing their own counsel, 5 using the legal counsels of other IGs' offices, and 1 using the legal resources of the IG Council.

IGs Reported Rarely Using the 7-Day Letter

The IG Act provides a reporting tool that can protect the independence of the IGs who report immediately to the agency head particularly serious or flagrant problems, abuses, or deficiencies relating the administration of programs or operations. The IG Act requires the agency head in turn to transmit the IG report, with the agency head's comments, to the appropriate committees or subcommittees of the Congress within 7 calendar days.

We asked whether any of the 62 IGs we surveyed had used the 7-day letter at any time during fiscal years 2008, 2009, and 2010. Only one, a presidentially appointed IG, had used the 7-day letter during this time frame. Specifically, on May 6, 2009, the IG delivered a report to the acting head under the IG Act provisions for a 7-day letter, in which the IG disagreed with the terms of a settlement reached by the agency with a grantee. The acting head provided the IG's report to the chairmen of numerous congressional committees on May 12, 2009, which was within the 7-day time frame. The IG's report gained the interest of congressional members and the issues were resolved by the President.

Generally, issues have been resolved more informally before getting to the point of using a 7-day letter. In 1999 we reported that no IGs had used the 7-

day letter during the period of January 1990 through April 1998.[13] In addition, we reported that a 10-year review of the IG Act by the House Committee on Government Operations in 1988 found that the IGs viewed the use of the 7-day letter as a last resort to attempt to force appropriate action by the agency.

Igs In DFEs with Boards and Commissions Generally Responded that the Dodd-Frank Act Provisions Enhance Independence

Provisions of the Dodd-Frank Act amending the IG Act are intended to provide an additional degree of independence to those IGs in DFEs with boards or commissions. Specifically, the Dodd-Frank Act provides that the head of the DFE[14] with a board or commission will be the board or commission and consequently, the IG appointment is no longer subject to the judgment of a single individual.[15] In addition, the Dodd-Frank Act requires the written concurrence of two-thirds of the members of these DFE boards and commissions for the removal or transfer of their IGs.

Twenty-six of the 33 DFE IGs are in DFEs with boards and commissions.[16] Of these 26 DFE IGs, 14 reported that the act's provision designating the boards and commissions as the DFE heads enhances their independence, and 20 responded that their independence is enhanced by requiring a two-thirds majority for their removal. A smaller number of affected IGs stated that these provisions had no effect on their independence, with 10 stating that the provision specifying the board or commission as the head had no effect and 5 reporting that the removal provision had no effect.

One DFE IG affected by the provisions did not respond to these survey questions. Also, a former DFE IG stated that reporting to his commission would reduce his independence because the commission has both federal and state members. However, the current IG who took office during our review stated that the primary concern is how nonfederal members would exercise their authority over a federal IG.

IG Budget Amounts Are Not Always Identified in the President's Budget Submissions

The Reform Act amended the IG Act to require that IG budget requests include certain information and be separately identified in the President's budget submission to the Congress. In addition, along with the separately identified IG budgets, the IGs may include comments with respect to the budget if the amount of the IG budget submitted by the agency or the President would substantially inhibit the IG from performing the duties of the office. These budget provisions are intended to help ensure adequate funding and additional independence of IG budgets by providing the Congress with transparency into the funding of each agency's IG while not interfering with the agency head's or the President's right to formulate and transmit their own budget amounts for the IG.

The fiscal year 2011 budget included amounts for 28 of the 30 presidentially appointed IGs. One presidentially appointed IG office was newly established and not included in the full fiscal year 2011 budget process. However another IG subject to these requirements did not have a specific budget amount separately disclosed in the President's budget. Of the 28 presidential IGs with budget amounts separately disclosed in the President's budget, 1 included comments indicating that the IG's fiscal year 2011 budget would substantially inhibit the IG from performing the duties of the office.

Regarding the DFE IGs, the President's budget had specific budget amounts for only 7 of the 33 DFE IGs. There were four newly established DFE IGs that were not part of the full fiscal year 2011 budget process. The President's budget did not contain specified budget amounts for the 22 remaining DFE IGs subject to these requirements. We notified the IG Council that most of the DFE IGs and one presidentially appointed IG did not have separate budget amounts included in the President's budget submission to the Congress. The IG Council has responded that it will review and assess this matter and, if necessary, work with congressional and administration officials to resolve this issue.

EFFECTIVENESS

The IGs' effectiveness was reflected in a range of reported accomplishments, such as potential dollars to be saved by the government through the results of federal IG audits, investigations, and other reports.[17] In addition, IG effectiveness was demonstrated in their efforts to help prevent fraud, waste, and abuse. For example, IGs in agencies receiving Recovery Act funds have reported providing oversight in the areas of establishing and maintaining controls to help ensure the funds are used properly. Also, the IGs' effectiveness was demonstrated by their reporting on oversight of management challenges identified at their agencies.

IGs Reported Significant Measurable Accomplishments

In their annual report to the President, the IGs established by the IG Act identified billions of dollars in savings and cost recoveries and other accomplishments resulting from their work in fiscal year 2009.[18] As part of this report for fiscal year 2009, these IGs identified $43.3 billion in potential savings from audits and investigations; and reported over 5,900 criminal actions, 1,100 civil actions, 4,460 suspensions or debarments, and over 6,100 indictments resulted from their work.[19] Based on this information, the potential dollar savings reported by these IGs represent a return on investment of approximately $18 for every IG dollar spent when compared to total IG fiscal year 2009 budget appropriations of $2.3 billion.

Recovery Board Reports of IG Effectiveness

In addition to measurable accomplishments, IGs also reported actions taken to prevent problems within their agencies, although these outcomes are more difficult to measure. For example, the IGs assisted in the oversight of expenditures authorized by the Recovery Act by reporting on preventive measures taken to help reduce the vulnerability of Recovery Act disbursements to fraud, waste, and abuse. The Recovery Act requires IG reviews of concerns raised by the public about investments of stimulus funds and provides IGs the authority to examine records and interview Recovery Act fund contractors and grantees. The Recovery Act established the Recovery Board whose members include 12 IGs and an additional IG as the chair, to coordinate and conduct oversight of funds distributed under the act in order to prevent fraud, waste, and abuse. In addition, the board is charged under the act with establishing and maintaining a user friendly website to foster greater accountability and transparency in the use of Recovery Act funds. To help prevent fraud and other potential wrongdoing, the IGs offered training to federal, state, and local employees, as well as contractors, private entities, and award recipients. The IGs' training was intended to improve awareness of the legal and administrative requirements of the Recovery Act programs.

As of June 2011, the Recovery Board reported that the IGs received over 7,000 complaints of wrongdoing associated with Recovery funds, opened over 1,500 investigations, and completed over 1,400 reviews of activities intended to improve the use of Recovery Act funds. In addition, the Recovery Board reported that IGs have provided over 2,000 training sessions to almost 139,000 individuals on the requirements of Recovery Act programs, how to prevent and report fraud, and how to manage grant and contract programs to meet legal and administrative requirements.

MANAGEMENT CHALLENGES EMPHASIZE AGENCY MISSION ISSUES

The management challenges reported annually by federal agencies in their performance and accountability reports along with relevant IG reports to address these challenges are key to focusing on effective IG oversight. The identification of management challenges by the IGs began in 1997 when congressional leaders asked the IGs to identify the 10 most serious management problems in their respective agencies. This request began a yearly process that continues as a result of the Reports Consolidation Act of 2000. This act calls for executive agencies to include their IGs' lists of significant management challenges in their annual performance and accountability reports to the President, the Office of Management and Budget, and the Congress.[20]

Not all agencies with IGs have requirements to report management challenges. Fifty-four of the IGs we surveyed reported having certain responsibilities for identifying management challenges in their agencies for fiscal year 2010. Through our survey, 27 of the IGs appointed by the President and 27 of the DFE IGs reported their agencies' management challenges and provided examples of audit reports that addressed about 90 percent of those challenges reported.

The responses from the IGs appointed by the President show that most of the 203 management challenges they reported for fiscal year 2010 focused on issues specific to their agencies' missions and performance management. (See fig. 1.) For example, the National Aeronautics and Space Administration's IG reported that major changes to the direction of the nation's space program present several management challenges, and the Department of Health and Human Services IG cited the management challenges associated with delivery of the nation's health care. The other management challenges addressed by the IGs relate to information technology, procurement, financial management, and human resources.

In addition, to provide oversight coverage of management challenges, the presidential IGs issued reports that addressed about 93 percent of the management challenges identified. These reports contained recommendations for improving the weaknesses specified by the management challenges. For example, the Federal Deposit Insurance Corporation IG recommended strengthening specific controls over managing the closing process for failed financial institutions which is a key aspect of FDIC's mission regarding insured depository institutions. Also, the Social Security Administration IG identified transparency and accountability issues as an agency management challenge and provided report recommendations for improved performance in this area.

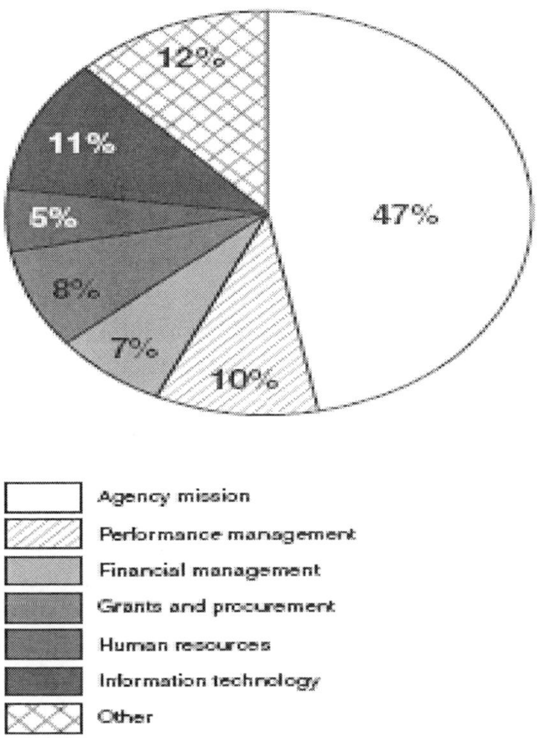

Source: GAO analysis of IG survey information.

Figure 1. Management Challenges Reported by IGs Appointed by the President.

The DFE IGs reported 124 management challenges for fiscal year 2010, with a focus on their agencies' missions, information technology, and performance management. (See fig. 2.) For example, the Farm Credit Administration's IG reported management challenges related to the safety, soundness, and mission accomplishment of the Farm Credit System. In addition, information technology, including information security, was often identified as a management challenge. For example, the Federal Maritime Commission's IG and the National Labor Relations Board's IG identified challenges in upgrading their agencies' management systems. The performance management issues the DFE IGs identified as management challenges included timely implementation of IG recommendations by the Peace Corps and expanding public access at the National Archives and Records Administration. The management challenges included in the "other" category included concerns over internal controls, improper payments, and the security of federal property.

In addition, the DFE IGs issued reports that addressed almost 90 percent of the management challenges identified and contained recommendations for corrective actions. For example, the Farm Credit Administration IG assessed the agency's readiness to take enforcement actions related to its mission. In another example, the Postal Service IG provided recommendations to improve the efficiency of postal operations related to performance management in sorting the mail.

Expertise

The 62 federal IGs responding to our survey reported information on their expertise and qualifications including the backgrounds, academic degrees, and professional certifications. The IGs' information showed a wide range of backgrounds, skills, and professional certifications relevant to their work consistent with the areas of demonstrated experience specified by the IG Act. Figure 3 summarizes the background experiences of the 62 IGs who responded to our survey. Most of the IGs appointed by the President reported that they had a background in criminal justice, investigations, law enforcement, and public administration, while most of the DFE IGs had backgrounds in inspections and evaluations, criminal justice, investigations, law enforcement, accounting and auditing, and financial analysis.

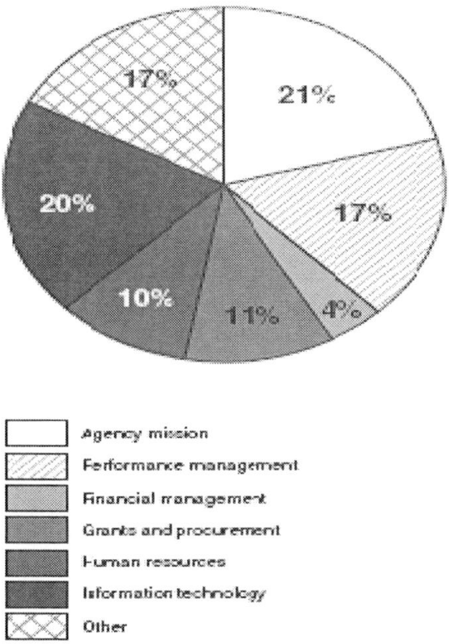

Source: GAO analysis of IG survey information.

Figure 2. Management Challenges Reported by DFE IGs.

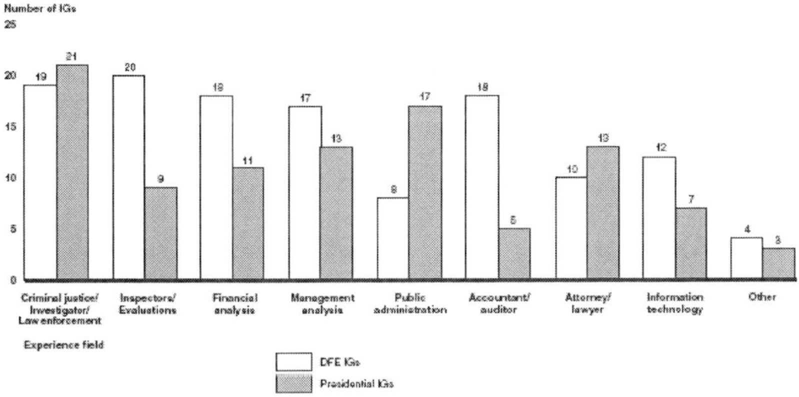

Source: GAO analysis of IG survey information.

Figure 3. Background Experience Reported by the IGs.

As summarized in figure 4, we also obtained information on the academic degrees obtained by the 62 IGs. Most of the IGs reported having degrees in areas that are relevant to performing in an IG position and in areas of demonstrated experience specified by the IG Act. To illustrate, 15 (about half of the IGs appointed by the President) had law degrees and 1 presidential IG had a degree in an accounting and auditing area. Twelve DFE IGs had law degrees and an equal number of DFE IGs had degrees in accounting and auditing related areas. Additional degrees were reported by both presidential and DFE IGs in areas of criminal justice, investigations, law enforcement; management analysis; and public administration. Other academic degrees reported by presidential and DFE IGs included mathematics, science, sociology, education, psychology, and English.

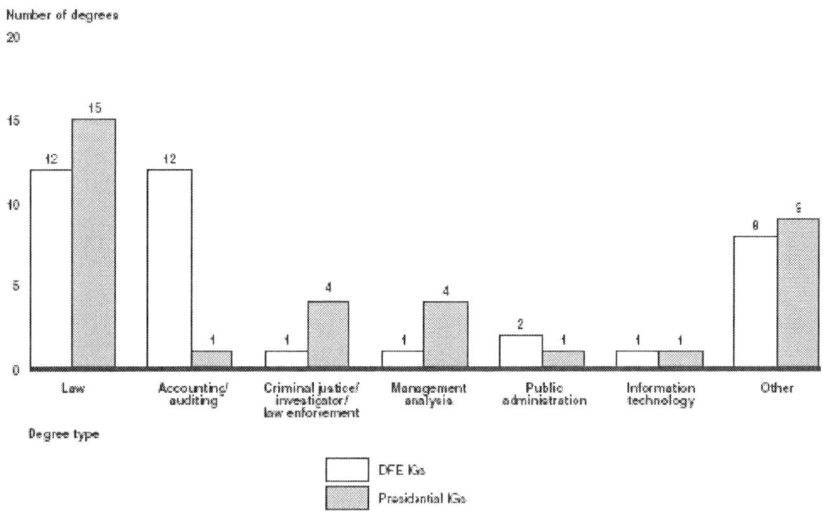

Source: GAO analysis of IG survey information.

Figure 4. Academic Degrees Held by the IGs.

With respect to professional certifications, 6 IGs appointed by the President reported having professional certifications and 28 DFE IGs reported they possessed at least one professional certification related to their IG responsibilities. For the presidential IGs, 2 were certified fraud examiners, 1 reported being a certified internal auditor, 1 reported being a certified government financial manager, and 2 had certifications in additional separate areas. Of the DFE IGs, 6 reported they are certified public accountants and 6 reported that they are certified internal auditors. Additional certifications reported by the DFE IGs include 6 certified government financial managers, 4 fraud examiners, 3 certified information systems auditors, and 7 with other certifications such as a certified government auditing professional, certified information security manager, certified information officer, and certified inspector general. (See fig. 5.)

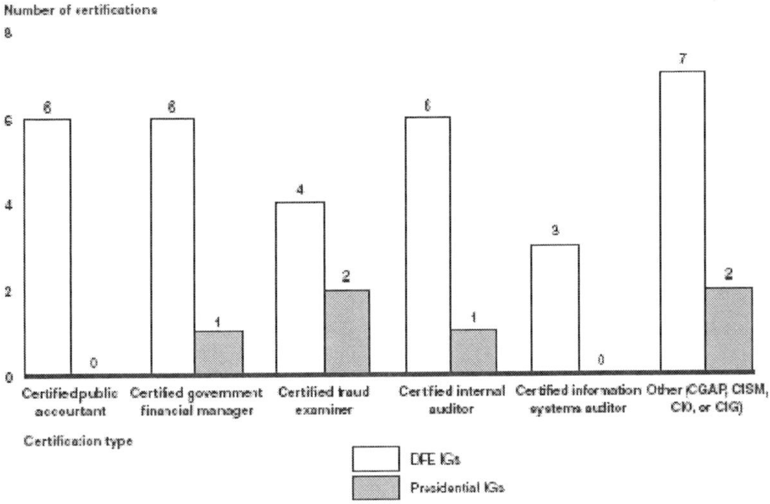

Source: GAO analysis of IG survey information.

Note:

CGAP = certified government auditing professional; CISM = certified information security manager; CIO = certified information officer; CIG = certified inspector general.

Figure 5. Certifications Held by the IGs.

AGENCY COMMENTS

We received comments from the IG Council (reprinted in app. V), on September 13, 2011. The council commented that the draft provided useful information on the independence, activities, and accomplishments of the federal inspectors general and, as such, will contribute to a greater understanding of the work of the IGs in providing oversight to a wide range of government programs. We also received, and incorporated as appropriate, technical comments from several IG offices.

Susan Ragland
Director, Financial Management and Assurance

List of Committees

The Honorable Joseph I. Lieberman
Chairman

The Honorable Susan M. Collins
Ranking Member
Committee on Homeland Security and Governmental Affairs
United States Senate

The Honorable Tim Johnson
Chairman

The Honorable Richard C. Shelby
Ranking Member
Committee on Banking, Housing, and Urban Affairs
United States Senate

The Honorable Darrell Issa
Chairman

The Honorable Elijah Cummings
Ranking Member
Committee on Oversight and Government Reform
House of Representatives

The Honorable Spencer Bachus
Chairman

The Honorable Barney Frank
Ranking Member
Committee on Financial Services
House of Representatives

APPENDIX I: DEPARTMENTS AND AGENCIES WITH INSPECTORS GENERAL[1]

1. Agency for International Development

2. Department of Agriculture
3. Department of Commerce
4. Corporation for National and Community Service
5. Department of Defense
6. Department of Education
7. Department of Energy
8. Environmental Protection Agency
9. Export-Import Bank of the United States
10. Federal Deposit Insurance Corporation
11. Federal Housing Finance Agency
12. General Services Administration
13. Department of Health and Human Services
14. Department of Homeland Security
15. Department of Housing and Urban Development
16. Department of the Interior
17. Department of Justice
18. Department of Labor
19. National Aeronautics and Space Administration
20. Nuclear Regulatory Commission
21. Office of Personnel Management
22. Railroad Retirement Board
23. Small Business Administration
24. Social Security Administration
25. Department of State
26. Tennessee Valley Authority
27. Department of Transportation
28. Department of the Treasury
29. Treasury Inspector General for Tax Administration
30. Department of Veterans Affairs

APPENDIX II: DESIGNATED FEDERAL AGENCIES WITH INSPECTORS GENERAL[1]

1. Amtrak
2. Appalachian Regional Commission
3. Commodity Futures Trading Commission
4. Consumer Product Safety Commission

5. Corporation for Public Broadcasting
6. Defense Intelligence Agency
7. Denali Commission
8. Election Assistance Commission
9. Equal Employment Opportunity Commission
10. Farm Credit Administration
11. Federal Communications Commission
12. Federal Election Commission
13. Federal Labor Relations Authority
14. Federal Maritime Commission
15. Federal Reserve Board
16. Federal Trade Commission
17. U.S. International Trade Commission
18. Legal Services Corporation
19. National Archives and Records Administration
20. National Credit Union Administration
21. National Endowment for the Arts
22. National Endowment for the Humanities
23. National Geospatial-Intelligence Agency[2]
24. National Labor Relations Board
25. National Reconnaissance Office
26. National Science Foundation
27. National Security Agency
28. Peace Corps
29. Pension Benefit Guaranty Corporation
30. Postal Regulatory Commission
31. U.S. Postal Service
32. Securities and Exchange Commission
33. Smithsonian Institution

APPENDIX III: AGENCIES AND OFFICES WITH INSPECTORS GENERAL ESTABLISHED BY VARIOUS STATUTES

1. Architect of the Capitol[1]
2. Central Intelligence Agency[2]
3. Government Accountability Office[3]

4. Government Printing Office[4]
5. Library of Congress[5]
6. Office of Director of National Intelligence[6]
7. Special Inspector General for Afghanistan Reconstruction[7]
8. Special Inspector General for Iraq Reconstruction[8]
9. Special Inspector General for the Trouble Asset Relief Program[9]
10. U.S. Capitol Police[10]

APPENDIX IV: DEPARTMENTS AND AGENCIES WITH ACT FDS INSPECTORS GENERAL RESPONSIBLE FOR OVERSIGHT OF RECOVERY ACT FUNDS

Agency for International Development

Amtrak

Corporation for National and Community Service

Department of Agriculture[1] Department of Commerce[1] Department of Defense[1] Department of Education[1] Department of Energy[1]

Department of Health and Human Services[1]

Department of Homeland Security[1]

Department of Housing and Urban Development

Department of Justice[1] Department of Labor Department of State Department of the Interior[1] Department of Transportation[1]

Department of the Treasury[1]

Department of the Treasury – Treasury Inspector General for Tax Administration[1]

Department of Veterans Affairs

Environmental Protection Agency

Federal Communications Commission

General Services Administration

National Aeronautics and Space Administration

National Endowment for the Arts

National Science Foundation

Office of Personnel Management

Railroad Retirement Board Small Business Administration

Smithsonian Institution

Social Security Administration

End Notes

[1] The Dodd-Frank Act was enacted in response to the near collapse of the U.S. financial system in September 2008, to improve oversight of the financial markets and make the financial system more sound, stable, and safer for consumers and investors. Pub. L. 111-203, 124 Stat. 1376 (July 21, 2010).

[2] Pub. L. No. 95-452, 92 Stat. 1101 (Oct. 12, 1978) codified, as amended, at 5 U.S.C. App.

[3] Pub. L. No. 100-504, 102 Stat. 2515 (Oct. 18, 1988).

[4] Pub. L. No. 110-409, 122 Stat. 4302 (Oct. 14, 2008).

[5] The IG Council was established by the Reform Act and consists mainly of IGs to address integrity, economy, and effectiveness issues that transcend individual government agencies and to increase the professionalism and effectiveness of personnel in the IG offices.

[6] Pub. L. No. 111-5, 123 Stat. 115 (Feb. 17, 2009).

[7] U.S. Government Printing Office, Establishment of Offices of Inspector and Auditor General in Certain Executive Departments and Agencies, Report of the Committee on Governmental Affairs United States Senate, Report No. 95-1071 (Washington, D.C.: Aug. 8, 1978).

[8] The 10 IGs established by other statutes are outside the scope of this report. Also, one DFE IG did not respond to our survey.

[9] We obtained information from the Council of the Inspectors General on Integrity and Efficiency, A Progress Report to the President: Fiscal Year 2009 (Washington, D.C.: Nov. 15, 2010). As of August 1, 2011, the IG Council was reviewing the fiscal year 2010 information of the IGs' accomplishments and the fiscal year 2009 information was the most current.

[10] Pub. L. No. 106-531 114 Stat. 2537 (Nov. 22, 2000).

[11] Twenty-six of the 33 DFE IGs are affected by the Dodd-Frank Act provisions because their DFEs have either boards or commissions. The 26 DFE IGs are a subset of the 62 IGs who responded to our survey.

[12] GAO, Inspectors General: Independence of Legal Services Provided to IGs, GAO/OGC-95-15 (Washington, D.C.: Mar. 1, 1995).

[13] GAO, Inspectors General: Information on Operational and Staffing Issues, GAO/AIMD-99-29 (Washington, D.C.: Jan. 4, 1999).

[14] The head of the DFE means the person or persons that the IG is under the general supervision of, for purposes of the IG Act, as amended.

[15] Where there is no board or commission, the head is the person or persons designated by statute or the chief policymaking officer if not defined in statute.

[16] The Dodd-Frank Act specifically designates the Council of the Arts as the head of the National Endowment for the Arts and the Council of the Humanities as the head of the National Endowment for the Humanities; therefore these IGs are included in our survey results.

[17] Potential savings reported by the IGs includes investigative receivables and actual recoveries.

1[8] In fiscal year 2009 there were 59 IG offices established by the IG Act.

[19] At least one IG refers to these reported accomplishments as "production figures."

[20] The Reports Consolidation Act requirements do not apply to all agencies with IGs; therefore, our survey obtained the management challenges as reported by 27 DFE IGs and 27 IGs appointed by the President.

End Note for Appendix I

[1] IGs established by the IG Act of 1978, as amended, with appointment by the President and Senate confirmation.

End Notes for Appendix II

[1] IGs established by the IG Act of 1978, as amended, with appointment by the agency head. In addition, the Department of State IG provides oversight of the Broadcasting Board of Governors, which is a designed federal entity.

[2] No responses were provided to our survey.

End Notes for Appendix III

[1] Consolidated Appropriations Act, 2008, Pub. L. No. 110-161, § 1301, 121 Stat 1844, 2240 (Dec. 26, 2007), classified at 2 U.S.C. § 1808 (appointed by the agency head in consultation with the Inspectors General of the Library of Congress, Government Printing Office, Government Accountability Office, and United States Capitol Police).

[2] Intelligence Authorization Act, Fiscal Year 1990, Pub. L. No. 101-193, § 801, 103 Stat 1701, 1711 (Nov. 30, 1989) codified at 50 U.S.C. § 403q (appointed by the President with Senate confirmation).

[3] Government Accountability Office Act of 2008, Pub. L. No. 110-323, § 5, 122 Stat 3539, 3543 (Sept. 22, 2008) codified at 31 U.S.C. § 705 (appointed by the agency head).

[4] Government Printing Office Inspector General Act of 1988, Pub. L. No. 100-504, § 201–206, 102 Stat 2515 (Oct. 18, 1988) codified at 44 U.S.C. § 3901–3903 (appointed by the agency head).

[5] Library of Congress Inspector General Act of 2005, Pub. L. No. 109-55, § 1307, 119 Stat 565, 582 (Aug. 2, 2005) classified at 2 USCA § 185 (appointed by the agency head).

[6] Intelligence Authorization Act for Fiscal Year 2010, Pub. L. No. 111-259, § 405, 124 Stat 2654, 2709 (Oct. 7, 2010) codified at 50 U.S.C. § 403-3h (appointed by the President with Senate confirmation, but an IG is not yet appointed).

[7] National Defense Authorization Act for Fiscal Year 2008, Pub. L. No. 110-181, § 1229, 122 Stat 3, 378 (Jan. 28, 2008) codified at 5 U.S.C. App. § 8G note (appointed by the President only).

[8] Emergency Supplemental Appropriations Act for Defense and for the Reconstruction of Iraq and Afghanistan, 2004, Pub. L. No. 108-106, § 3001, 117 Stat 1209, 1234 (Nov. 6, 2003) as amended by Ronald W. Reagan National Defense Authorization Act for Fiscal Year 2005, Pub. L. No. 108-375, § 1203, 118 Stat 1811, 2078 (Oct. 28, 2004) codified at 5 U.S.C. App. § 8G (appointed by the Secretary of Defense in consultation with the Secretary of State).

[9] Emergency Economic Stabilization Act of 2008, Pub. L. No. 110-343, § 121, 122 Stat 3765, 3788 (Oct. 3, 2008) codified at 12 U.S.C. § 5231 (appointed by the President with Senate confirmation).

[10] Legislative Branch Appropriations Act, 2006, Pub. L. No. 109-55, § 1004, 119 Stat 565, 572 (Aug. 2, 2005) classified at 2 U.S.C. § 1909 (appointed by agency head in consultation with

the Inspectors General of the Library of Congress, Government Printing Office, and the Government Accountability Office).

End Note for Appendix IV

[1] The IG is a member of the Recovery Accountability and Transparency Board.

INDEX

A

B

C

D

E

Q

R

S

T

V

W